England

Poems from a School

England

Poems from a School

Edited by Kate Clanchy

PICADOR

First published 2018 by Picador
an imprint of Pan Macmillan
20 New Wharf Road, London N1 9RR
Associated companies throughout the world
www.panmacmillan.com

ISBN 978-1-5098-8660-9

Visit **www.picador.com** to read more about all our books
and to buy them. You will also find features, author interviews and
news of any author events, and you can sign up for e-newsletters
so that you're always first to hear about our new releases.

For Helen Beech and Christine Atkinson,

Miss B and Miss A,

teachers without stint or par,

without whom this book would not exist.

I Want a Poem

I want a poem
with the texture of a colander
on the pastry.

A verse
of pastry so rich
it leaves gleam on your fingertips.

A poem
that stings like the splash of boiling oil
as you drop the pastry in.

A poem
that sits on a silver plate with
nuts and chocolates, served up to guests who
sit cross legged on the *thoshak*.

A poem
as vibrant as our saffron tea
served up at Eid.

Let your poetry
texture the blank paper
like a prism splitting light.

Don't leave without seeing all the colours.

Shukria Rezaei (18)

Contents

[*x*]

Introduction

The poems in this anthology are too fresh, too moving and too compelling for any reader to be studying my words first. I am writing this introduction, then, on the assumption that you have read at least a handful of them, and want the answers to a couple of burning questions: are these poems really by teenagers, and why are they so good?

So first of all: these poems were – genuinely – all written by school pupils aged between eleven and nineteen, and all in the same small school, Oxford Spires Academy, over the last eight years while I have worked there as Writer in Residence. Quite often, I watched early versions being scrawled out on the library table at our after-school workshops; always, I saw drafts and redrafts tapped out on school computers. They were not written by especially 'academic' children, and certainly not by rich or privileged ones. All the poets here come from striving migrant families and several are refugees. Nor is Oxford Spires Academy, despite its aspirational name, a hothouse or even a selective school: it's a comprehensive in the poverty-stricken east of the sprawling, industrial, un-dreamy conurbation of Oxford, well out of sight of the famous spires.

OSA does have one special characteristic, though: its ethnic mix. It is the chosen school of Oxford's many migrants, both for the asylum-seeking families who come in from nearby Heathrow and Campsfield, and for the 'economic migrants' who man the city's huge hospitals and thriving car plant. For most of my years at OSA, the school has had only about 20% White British pupils. The other 80% are Nepalese and Brazilian, Tanzanian and Lithuanian, Korean and Swedish, pupils from every part of India and every country in Europe; refugees from conflict, and refugees from poverty; kids from Algeria, Somalia, Kosovo, Albania, Afghanistan, and most recently, Syria. Our school speaks more than thirty languages, maybe fifty dialects. This creates something magical – a community without a majority culture or religion, and a mix so extreme that no one can disappear into their own cultural grouping: everyone has to make friends, companions, and enemies across racial and language divides.

So our class registers are gloriously confounding, with names ranging from Alkaida to Urban, Swostika to Lunch. If you were to walk round our school on a sunny afternoon, you might pass a basketball player called Jesus (from São Paulo), tossing the ball to Mohammed (from Afghanistan); a six-foot Somali girl swapping prom dress designs with her best friend, a five-foot white-blonde girl from Poland; a girl in hijab from Syria holding hands with another from Iran, and sharing her cherries, as if neither had ever heard of the Sunni–Shia divide. It's a beautiful, tender, comical sight: I never tire of it. I don't think the staff do either. Certainly, what they lovingly call 'the kids, our kids, our lot, just the kids really', seem to draw and retain a remarkably dedicated band of teachers.

And it also creates a special sort of openness. There is no one culture, here, no single idea of what a school should be; so if the teachers tell them – as in OSA we do – that a school is a haven of equality and kindness, a place where everyone tries (as the school motto naively, sweetly, truthfully, asserts) 'to be the best they can be' . . . They actually believe us. In OSA we also have conspired to tell them that girls are good at football; that the library is the most important place in the school; and that poetry is for everyone.

We show our pupils that is normal to write poetry regularly (the Head Girl does it, and the most prestigious sixth-formers), publish it in little books, and read it aloud in all sorts of places. We teach them – and it is a 'we', for my work would be nowhere and nothing without the support, year in year out, of the school's remarkable English Department – that poetry is also their school's top sport, the one in which OSA students have, for the last five years, won more prizes in national competitions than any other in the UK; and, in the same way that Eton school boys ready themselves for Cabinet, they believe us and make it true again.

So that is one reason why our poems are so good: we, as a school, expect and believe that they can be, and as a school we support their creation. That's a big reason: it is impossible to overstate how profound and multi-layered are the forces of cultural silencing, or how strong and subtle is the belief that poetry belongs only to the privileged. I believe, too, that though my school has an especially tender culture, and an alchemy inherent in its ethnic mix, that any school which sincerely set out to do so and was able to make the investment could produce similarly confident writers, and put poetry at the heart of its teaching.

But not all schools could produce a book like this, because there is another factor at work here: that of language loss and change. The poets represented here all came to English, or at least written English, late, after they were six: each student here, whether because of migration, deafness, or dyslexia, went through a period when they lost their native language, and, as Rukiya Khatun so movingly puts it, 'silence itself was my friend'. That locked-down period may be painful, but it feeds the inner voice. I think it may also account for the musicality of so many of these poems: unlike adults, children can learn another language without an accent, because their ears and brains are still open to all the sounds and rhythms of another speech, so when these young people hear a poem in English (and that is all we do in my workshops: read a poem, then write one) they hear all its sounds, and can reproduce them as fluently as they can an English accent.

These young poets all have another language at their shoulder: a mother tongue. The shapes of that language show through their English. That is part of their freshness and originality, much in the way that passing a simple metaphor through Google Translate, and back again, may turn it into poetry. But the word 'mother' also matters: it is no coincidence that all the poets here had at least one story-telling, poem-singing, non-English speaking, magical parent. When I started a Ghazal Club with Arabic, Bengali, Urdu and Farsi speaking students, and explained this ancient form, one of the Afghan girls said: 'I didn't know that ghazals were proper poems. I thought it was just something my mum knew.' But her illiterate, brilliant mother knew, as so many Afghan women do, how to use pictures and sound to tell a salty story, create comedy and set a memory, and she had passed that ability to her daughter, who passed it into English. That gift shines through in Azfa Awad's tales of Tanzania, or Shukria Rezaei's Rumi-derived odes: the capacity to sing an image.

And perhaps that most ancient purpose of poetry – to remember – is also at the root of the power of this anthology. The poems here are about lost countries, because wherever my workshops began – with a Simon Armitage poem perhaps, or one by Lorraine Mariner, set in Yorkshire or Essex – my students found themselves remembering their own lost homes. And when they did, they also found themselves writing at their best, as more than themselves, with their home tongues pressing in their mouths, their magical mothers at their shoulders. These poems are like the psalms sung by the rivers of Babylon, to remember home in a strange land: something very old. But they are also something very new – poems made in a new English, one inflected by all the poets' languages, all their poetries and gifts, and by the mass migration of the twenty-first century. These poems are charged with excitement because they were written as England changed, on the cutting edge of that change; and, for all the sadness they record, they are joyous because they are about living in that new England, a country founded on second chances, tolerance, kindness, and luck, a country they see in their eccentric, loving, striving school, a country that, whatever the difficulties, these young people already love.

KATE CLANCHY,
Writer in Residence,
Oxford Spires Academy

England

I had seen it
in photographs,
I could not imagine it.
How were the days?
What were they filled with?
Roosters crowing

needlessly?
Or perhaps
the remains
of summer grass steaming,
musty but familiar.
Was the now searing sun ripe there?

Would the buds grow,
from season to season?
Would the lemon trees
kindle,
in the light,
or the pigmy bananas flourish?

Then,
I set out to be a woman,
fearless of the natives,
Down There;
In that world.
Not mine.

Rukiya Khatun (17)

War Memoir

I was five years old,
hiding under the bed,
listening to the footsteps
of approaching soldiers
who had weapons
that could tear my limbs
like a lion's jaw.

But I was strong.
I breathed in the dusty air
and screamed 'STOP THE WAR!'

I may have been small
but when trapped
between the claws of war
my voice could soar:
sound like the bangs and cracks
spat by the tongues of fireworks;

And when I ran
away from their biting guns,
my feet could dance,
skim above rose petals
dripping from my toes.

Azfa Awad (18)

To Make a Homeland

Can anyone teach me
how to make a homeland?
Heartfelt thanks if you can,
heartiest thanks,
from the house-sparrows,
the apple-trees of Syria,
and yours very sincerely.

Amineh Abou Kerech (13)

A Glass of Tea

(after Rumi)

Last year, I held a glass of tea to the light. This year,
I swirl like a tealeaf in the streets of Oxford.

Last year, I stared into navy blue sky. This year,
I am roaming under colourless clouds.

Last year, I watched the dazzling sun dance gracefully. This year,
the faint sun moves futurelessly.

Migration drove me down this bumpy road,
where I fell and smelt the soil, where I arose and sensed the cloud.

Now I am a bird, flying in the breeze,
lost over the alien earth.

Don't stop and ask me questions.
Look into my eyes and feel my heart.

It is bruised, aching and sore.
My eyes are veiled with onion skin.

I sit helplessly in an injured nest,
not knowing how to fix it.

And my heart, I'd say
is displaced

struggling to find its place.

Shukria Rezaei (18)

The Doves of Damascus

I lost my country and everything I had before.
and now
I cannot remember for sure

the soft of the snow in my country,
I cannot remember
the feel of the damp air in summer.

Sometimes I think I remember
the smell of jasmine
as I walked down the street.

And sometimes autumn
with its orange and scarlet leaves
flying in the high Damascus sky.

And I am sure I remember
my grandmother's roof-garden,
its vines, its sweet red grapes,

the mint she grew in crates for tea.
I remember the birds, the doves
of Damascus. I remember

how they scattered.
I remember
trying to catch them.

Ftoun Abou Kerech (14)

I Don't Remember

I don't remember the place
where the only colour I saw was green.
Where the blazing heat would challenge me –
not even the tall twisty trees
they tell me I used to climb.

I have forgotten
the mangy dogs I used to bark at
and the snakes I waited to pelt rocks at,
the fish I caught by hand –
even the dragonflies I trapped.

I have forgotten the taste
of the just ripe mangoes
which I would climb the trees to pick,
and of fresh fish too big to fit
in the kitchen; and of the chickens
slaughtered in front of me, and
of the birds, sling-shotted from the sky,
which would all end up in a pot filled with spices
which would soon be empty unless I got there first . . .

I don't remember the taste of dried dates
from the market, the peaches, the jackfruit,
the pineapples, the juiciness of it all.
I don't remember the smells,
the market filled with men chatting,
waiting for a customer,
or of the cut grasses being stored
for all that livestock.

I don't remember the view from those
huge hills which were so hard to climb.
Or the eagles soaring high in the sky waiting
to pull something out of the green.
Or the cows grazing on the grass,
all year continuously munching, munching away,
not even the painted fences in their neat rows.

No, I don't remember the day my life
was taken away.
I don't remember the fearless boy I used to be.
I don't remember my country . . .
Bangladesh.

Ismail Akthar (12)

[7]

The Return

No smell of fruit and marble floors, no
swirling noises of fans, no
animals, nothing
that felt alive.

No clear water, springs, no
fresh fruit high off the trees.
No huge balconies on top
of even higher houses where
we could laze around in the sun –
nothing of the sort, here.

The first noise back was the key in the lock.
The start of my updated life.

Maah-Noor Ali (15)

Homesick

There is that strange smell again, the tang of
the cars on the road screeching, not like
the laborious rickshaw in Bangladesh. There is no
inviting market, no smell of spices and sliced fruit.

Look ahead, jump, skip and hop. Hide the fact
you are alienated. Chew on the candy floss.
It melts in your mouth. Such foreign stuff!
There are cracks on the pavement: you tiptoe.

Look up, the sky is blue. Here, the same
clouds appear, but nothing is the same.

Rukiya Khatun (16)

Torun

I come from Torun,
from the ancient landmarks,
the bakeries which release
their odours onto the streets.

I come from the damp rainy
days which flood England.
I come from a grandfather
who is not related yet I
call my own.

I come from the tunes
of an accordion all the way
from Poland. I come from
the meowing and moaning of my cats,
from the loving of my mum and dad.

I come from the car fumes
which corrupt your lungs.
I come from the vast blue sky
which eats your eyes as you stare at it.
I come from Poland.

Miron Bartowski (13)

How to Forget Your Mother's Language

First – you learn that you will never be your mother or your father.

You will never inherit the rebellion of your father's youth or the burn of the church school's ruler along his white-red wrists.

You will never inherit the childhood chores of your mother; nor the heavy eyelids during 5 a.m. devotional prayers. You will never thank God for the sun, the same glaring sun that bullied her into parched brown-red skin. You will never pray for rain: not the warm rain of South East Asia's summers, but cool English rain.

Then, you learn how to talk. You will grow up in your father's home, with your father's language. You learn that it is almost impossible to understand your mother in the words she used to live in. You listen to her phone calls, and you hear the unfamiliar rhythm of her words. It is not fragmented like when she speaks your father's language. It makes you feel misplaced. You only understand your name, but that name is lost in the middle of her sentences, along with the rhythm and the other crackly voice.

You understand it feels better to rest against your father's chest. You listen to his phone calls, understanding that it's a call to Uncle David, and that your father wants his help painting the fence. You feel the phonetic patterns resonate from his chest, the familiar rhythm you grew up with.

But you remind yourself that you are neither your father nor your mother.

You understand your father's language was not inherited, the same way that his childhood troubles are not part of your disposition. You understand that it is easy to forget the rhythm, or the words, of your mother's language. You understand that she, too, forgets yours.

Sophie Dunsby (17)

My Hazara People

I can't write about my Hazara people,
who have suffered for decades
in Afghanistan where they come from
in Pakistan where they are murdered,
In Iran where they offend
because of their almond shaped eyes.
My mind is blank!

I can't write about how loud the shooting was
just two miles away from my house,
how my aunt fainted,
how nervous my mom got,
how the cup fell from her hand.

I can't write about how innocent people died:
how the Martyr's necropolis gets bigger and bigger;
how my people suffer;
how cruel this world can get;
how frightening it is

for kids like me.

Shukria Rezaei (15)

Jasmine

My name is the white flower, and maybe a whiff of the Roaring Twenties music that horrified sniffers in walnut church pews. My name is Classic and English and at school they call me Jasmine B, or JB, or – horror of horrors – Justin Bieber, to distinguish me from the other Jasmines.

My mum says I am Jasmine because, when she met her father, there were jasmine flowers around the door. He was the only one of her family who loved her. Her mother hated her, and yelled once, "We don't want coffee coloured people here!" and so Mum changed her name from Susan to Sushila.

I am named after the jasmine flowers around my Indian grandfather's door, but there isn't spice in my name; just white scent. Jasmine is a safe name, a scared name, a coward's choice.

Jasmine Burgess (14)

Eyen

The way you looked at me with those round misty eyes, and your wide nose and your bright pink lips.

How you stood with your size three feet supporting a five-foot-five frame.

When Mum left I would wake up every morning crying to the little picture I had of her, and you would take it away from me and hold me close to say, *Don't worry, she's out there for you.*

You never asked for anything. You sacrificed your own education because your father couldn't afford to send two girls to school, and chose my mother. But you would have been bright.

When you dressed me in my uniform you would whisper in my ear: *Eyen comeyen abasi ke nfo:* Child, I thank God for you.

Michael Egbe (17)

Missing Proofing Tools

This text
contains text
in Hungarian
which isn't
being

Proofed.

You may
be able
to get
proofing tools
for this

Language.

Download.

Never Show

Again.

Vivien Urban (17)

Where Are My Unnumbered Days?

Once I lived in a beautiful town;
Once, I owned a beautiful house,
with a grand garden full of flowers,
and I was prince of it all. Once,
I lived in a house with a name:

And now, I am just a number.
Nations talked to nations
and robbed me of myself.
They made me
a number among millions.

But my rights have no number.
My home had no number.
I could not count the petals of the flowers.
My childhood in the garden
had no limits on it.

Take me back to my country
and I can show you the numbers.
The numbers who suffer.
The quantities of beauty.
The fallen flowers.

Mohamed Assaf (12)

Это не трамвай!

This isn't a tram!
My mother cries.
Закрой двери!
My mother says.
Shut the doors!

I imagine a tram. A tram
at the end of the line,
screeching rusty tracks,
a soft wind filtering
its fading interior,
a metallic bulky haul
of emptiness.

This tram only stops
when the doors slam shut.
So this tram never stops.
And this tram has no more tracks.

Now our living room is full
of Russia.
And still, it is not a tram.

Anton Chrapovikij (18)

Mother Triptych

My mother smokes

I mumble to the dish platter, the rice,
stuck like mash to the porcelain plate.
I hear her behind the door
behind the gushing of the water,
the lasting traces of curry, crying,
weathered. I mumble faster now,
gibbets of German cutting
the air, punishing, snapping.

There is water on my phone.
The screen reflects the vastness
of space, capturing light, frozen, a paradigm
of giga-bytes and square roots of infinity, time
multiplied by time, database subtracted by life.
What are you saying she says,
at last, and I tell her that she is
the spark on her own cigarette and

eventually the toxin will settle.

My mother asks me: 'Am I funny?'

Ma Hassutdo Chu? Am I funny?
The phrase is heavier indoors.
Dry scented tips of bamboo sticks
embed themselves on her tongue.

Don't I make you laugh? It's the
sound of doubt, like rising oxygen
wobbled by heat. In Nepalese
adjectives have cases.

***

In English, I laugh
at broken glass, or
azure chewing gum, sticking
to double ends. In Nepalese

laughter is air trapped
in a silk purse, gold and
autumnal, or cupped
in hands like chicken feet.

Year-grated hands, worked and rough.
In Nepalese, *laugh* is a non-reflexive verb.

My mother screams

And that day, just living
beat me up with its fluid limbs.

And that day, fear sucked the vapour
from my lungs and my heart fell into pieces,

And that day my tongue moved
of its own accord, at sixteen beats per minute.

And that day, I let fly my white flags,
and she opened my flood gates to pity.

And that day I heard the plopping sound of a body.
And the muffled screams through the tiles.

And that day I heard her.
I heard her, I heard her,
I hear her.

Mukahang Limbu (15)

Aashak/Ravioli

I hear our teapot pop as the lid is pulled.
It's time to unwrap my legs and get
my bottom off the *thoshak*
I enter the kitchen with a sigh:
her baggy, wrinkled sleeves are rolled up,
the short hairs on her arms dusted in flour.
Soft dough is squelched against the thin metal bowl,
until it's hard enough to crackle like nutshell.
Life moulds you in soft and hard shapes.

She lays the handmade towel gently on the table.
The thin wooden rolling pin runs
over the dough now wider than her arms.
The bowl full of finely chopped leek
beside her, waiting to be
mixed with spices and herbs,
locked in a different world.
Life is full of ups and downs.

She shouts: *Get your hands moving!*
I pick up the thin dough circle,
Shaking off the excess flour
to heap helplessly on my slippers.

I begin filling in each circle, closing
the edges with my fingertips. Letting
each one go into an ocean of boiling water . . .
Steam-filled kitchen, choking me.

She inspects.
The edges aren't closed fully, it's opened.
Life is an ocean, if you swim
you will reach your destination.
Otherwise, it will pop your insides out.

Shukria Rezaei (18)

Not this year Grandma

Aisha! says my Columbian grandmother,

Aisha, your ears need piercing.
She inspects
the two
pure ovals
on the side of my head,

and I picture her
among my disapproving aunts,
needle like a sword,
apple like a shield
in her hands

and suddenly
as if she had tapped a baton
on a sheet of music
it starts: *Are you a girl?*
Girl? Girl?

Yes, I say and now
only my brother
can save me
but next year he won't be so cute

and the needle will still be waiting.

Aisha Borja (14)

My Poem is a Jackfruit

The smell of it clings.
And the inside feels
like the gooey ink
that my brother puts
in his red car engine.

It is tough as wood,
scaly as a dinosaur.
But inside, soft as wool.
And the taste is
sweet heavens,
the world's greatest foods
having a party.

My poem doesn't walk
but it rolls.
It doesn't talk
but it sits there,
and the look of it
tells you that it doesn't want
to be touched or picked up
because it can prick your finger
and put you to sleep.

Emee Begum (16)

Silence Itself

When I was at school, I wanted a friend.
I feared being alone, not because
I minded the being alone, just
people pitying my loneliness.

When I was at school,
I never bothered to say anything:
secretly I think I was
satisfied with the silence.

When I was at school, I preferred
To watch the others playing.
That was fun enough.
And perhaps silence itself

was my friend, when I was at school.
I know I always felt like a ghost:
observing the world, and myself,
as if we were worth observing.

Rukiya Khatun (17)

I Come From

I come from the streets
that replaced grass and flowers
with concrete and syringes;

I come from grey flats towering,
injecting venom into the sky's blue skin.

I come from salty tears
running down his stubbled chin.
gorilla hands,
stained from building car parts.
Factory work.
The one-way ticket to a better future.

I come from
manky dishes
stained mattresses,
white walls dripping
with the damp, brown
smell of poverty.

I come from school:
the education system
that gives me a pen
only to poke myself blind with,

I come from insanity:
from catching falling stars
born of the pregnant night:
aflame with dreams and poetry.

Azfa Awad (17)

Clouds

When I was a child
I had no idea how day and night worked.
I thought, when it was night here
it was night worldwide,
and the same thing with the day.

I thought cloud was made
of cotton wool, and someday
I would go there, and grab a piece
of white, of the mysterious shapes
I saw when I looked up at the sky.

But when I was a child I also
thought I would become a doctor,
with all that strange equipment and
a stethoscope round my neck and
glasses on the end of my nose.

And now I am grown up, I know
it is impossible to grab that piece of cloud.
And as for me becoming a doctor –
the only thing lacking
is my knowledge of all doctor subjects.

Emee Begum (16)

Cape

When I was a kid, I was always waiting for that freak accident,
the one that would cause the awesome explosion that
would spread gamma rays down my blood stream; for that
rush, that rage, as my cells fused with this strange element.

I could see myself on a hospital bed surrounded
by doctors unable to explain the marvel I am.
I knew I would feel no pain as a needle tried
to pierce my skin, impenetrable as a turtle's shell,

and that soon I'd wake up and see my flabs
turn to abs, my biceps bulge out of my sleeves
and I'd try to walk but end up defying gravity and –
quickly forgetting how terrified of heights I am –

slip into that skin-tight costume with the silky cape
that moves and rustles with the wind
as I stand at the top of the Empire State Building
glaring into the clear blue sky, and

(momentarily ignoring the beautiful brunette reporter
who was going to fall deeply in love with me
when I revealed my mysterious secret identity to her
and asked her to be my bride)

swoop down to the street to that small fat kid
who'd just been dipped in the toilet by his high-school bullies
and give him courage to fight back not with violence
but with the aim to change them for the better, and

fly him around in my cape and tell him that I've got him.

Michael Egbe (17)

Sorrow Poem

Drinking the richness of my sorrows,
these salty tears turn my tongue green.
So when I speak,
I spit acid remarks
at my mother
who is ill.

I'm cleaning up my brother's sick:
yellow slime
with orange bits:
all over my flower-print
duvet cover.
Now my delicate brown
hand is gloved with yolk.

With stinging eyes,
I wipe the pains
from the ground,
rinse them into the past,

hang my eyes on the thread of hope,
turn to the sun,
and with the motion of the wind,
pray that they blink me
into a brighter future.

Azfa Awad (16)

Homesick

Today, I thought of my mud house:
the rough walls standing tall;
the fresh smell of clay on the floor;
the scraping of dirt from my shoes.

Today I remembered my school:
the straight marching lane up and down;
the fresh milk in my back pack
churning to butter as I marched.

Today I remembered my outdoor bathing:
the thick stream of water
gushing down on my head;
my mother's warning about the current's force.

Today I missed the jagged roads.
The horizons of mountains looming
with calming familiarity.
The way the sky flowered.
The way I used to live.

Shukria Rezaei (18)

Sylhet

There,
sun birds chipper;
Their feathers, light lime,
seep in the sunshine.

Crisp leaves grow,
wild and olive,
and the silent streams
run,

fresh water,
to guide the Elish,
silver, simple fish,
away to the sea.

Mango trees
summit and soar,
stalk high above
the forest floor

where
a Bengal tiger,
obsolete
as an emperor

trembles
as the hushed wind –
breathes –

Rukiya Khatun (16)

Hungary

Look,
at these flat lands
before you. Endless sky
fills empty space.
Stand here,
and open up your mind.
Notice the light
riding on its cloud horse
throwing shadows
on the grassy ground.
Stand here
and hear the whistle of the wind
blowing the golden sand.
Remember it,
elsewhere,
the free and wild wind,

as a gentle touch.

Vivien Urban (14)

Directions

You know, the traffic light in the middle of the Cowley Road, with an old man sitting on a white chair, smoking and staring? And in front of it is a bus stop with long queues and impatient people, and the road is thin and long with two different names, Oxford Road and Cowley Road, and busy cars and bicycles and buses going past?

This is not home.

You know the high rocky mountains with a jagged road, and the mud houses down the valley with sheep, goats, chickens and cows in their stables all lowing and waiting to be fed? And in front of the house is a woman chopping up grass so fresh that the smell clings to your nose as you pass by? And when you enter the house that smells of peace and love you are heartily welcomed and invited to tea and borsagh, and kishmish nakhut –

This is my home.

Shukria Rezaei (16)

The Cowley Road

So, wandering and wondering, I have ended up at the Cowley Road, aka the Road of Nationalities. Sometimes it seems as if every part of the world has gathered here: Polish, Pakistani, Italian, Greeks; the list goes on but I do not wish to.

Somehow it's the worst kind of busy; enough to hear the shouts of conversations buzzing in my ear (a straight lane to a headache) but not busy enough for it all to blend.

At the top of Cowley Road, your senses are flooded. Each of them. Sensory overload. It's as if the colours of the people's personalities are reflected in their clothes; and the smells are overwhelming. Because there are so many, you cannot focus on a specific one. International cuisine. Fast food. Cheap perfume. Smoke: significantly; a lot. And rubbish: bins litter the various lanes springing out of the main road.

Sound is peculiar. As a child all I used to hear was passing conversation and joyous shouts of my friends across the road or just ahead of me. Now I hear the dangerous rush of cars on the overcrowded road. I hear music I dislike blaring out of certain shops and worst of all I hear the whispers of middle-aged men who leer. I force myself to walk up the pavement though, wishing I wasn't so self-conscious that it seems as if the whole road were out to get me. To curl me up in its tentacles and swallow me whole.

The Cowley Road: never anyone's actual destination; just a small passage in a big book.

Asima Qayyum (17)

How not to be Korean

한국인이 되지 않는 법.

Hangug-in doeji anhneun beob.

Live in a country where you are the minority.
당신이 소수인 나라에 산다.
Dangsin-I sosu-in nala-e sanda.

Where a finger pointing in your direction is as common as a handshake.
당신의 방향 가리키는 손가락은 악수만큼 흔하다.
Dangsin-ui banghyang-eul galikineun songalag-eun agsumankeum
heunhada.

Where you would be lucky enough to receive a bow.
활을받을 정도로 우니 좋을 것이다.
Hwal-eulbad-eul jeongdolo uni-I joh-eul geos-ida.

Han Sun Nkumu (17)

I Have Divided My Heart,

and half of it is still in Syria.
When the sun shines in Syria
the warmth flowers in my cheek.

And when the sun sets there
my heart remembers shadows
and the closing of flowers.

Mohamed Assaf (12)

Time

For Jaferan Rehman and i.m. Abdul Rehman (2007)

We left before I had time,
before I had time to say,
to say I wasn't sure;
wasn't sure if it was the right choice,
the right choice to leave our home.
The home, the country, the place I lived in,
I lived in for all my life.
My life which was spent,
spent travelling back and forth,
back and forth, from England to Pakistan;
to Pakistan where we were going,
going to spend the rest of our lives.
The lives we imagined
imagined to be perfect,
perfect forever until,
until one day he left us.
Left us without giving me a chance,
a chance to say goodbye.
A goodbye which would have changed reality,
the reality we had to face and see,
had to see Ammi suffer,
suffer and cope and fight for hope,
hope to have one day fulfilled her duty,
her duty he gifted her for us,
for us so we could have the life we wanted,

We wanted then to come back to England,
England where our home was.
The home where we were expecting to see him again,
again live the normal life we had,
the normal life which included him.

Him without whom our lives were a question mark.

Rabia Rehmen (17)

Ghazal: Wings

I saw that I had been transformed into a crow with wings.
There were feathers black as death along my wings.

Why, said crow-girl, why are my feathers black, colour of death?
Where are the white feathers that covered my wings?

I am flying high above my country, over the Hindu Kush
mountains, over my village, on my wings.

I see the grey landscape, the grey towns, the green trees
near the mountains. I feel the dry wind under my wings.

I see the grave of my father, who I never knew,
I, Halema, on my black wings.

Halema Malak (14)

Papa,

There is a picture of you
   in this poem.
It is a photo of your face,
ripped from the album.
Your face   washed,
sepia coloured – the colour
of a cigar stubbed out on a sunset.

And this
is the only picture of you,
   Holding me up . . .

       You,

         Must,

           Have,

            Smelt,

           Like,

         Me.

Like baby milk –
Like lips just born.

This is the only place you are allowed to be.
  In this poem.

Papa.

        Mukahang Limbu (16)

I Can't Tell

I can't tell if a snowdrop will survive,
torn from its womb of soil, I don't know
if the snow angel will melt beside it.

Long gone are the days that wore out
grandmother's dress and her lost silk scarf
might never be worn again. I look up and see

airplanes cross, day by day miles and miles
of ocean giving back or taking a life.
And I know that the cherry tree in blossom

will shake its load, a rain of sweet scent
below onto the ground like a light,
soothing blanket. And when years from now

the remnants of a crown are discovered;
the lost piece of our grandmother's grace
will return to the grave

and her angel, long stripped from her wings, will fly.

Vivien Urban (17)

My Martyr Brother

أخي الشهيد

My martyr brother, you are going out of life.
Now you are lying in my heart and splitting me into pain.

Do you hear me, my eyes?
Eyes, will you come and witness this world with me?
For you are still alive. You are not a symbol.
You will not bend from hope. You will light
the fire of my revolution, but cannot light my brother.

Now my pen bleeds for him. Now I regret.
There are tears in my eyes.

*

I will never forget the paradise of the highest paradise, Lord.
I will never forget the paradise of the supreme paradise, Lord.
Brother, Our Lord will be your dwelling place
and your last home and my prayer.
Lord, grant that I may bless you again.
Lord, grant that our deaths may gather us together
in a testimony for the freedom of our land.

*

My brother, on one date, wait for me.

Einas Hadla (18)

The word Ummī – My Mother

My beloved mother.
When I go to my house, the pain of missing her
Arrives before me.

شعر عن الام

امي الغالية العزيزة، لما كنت أذهب إلى البيت و الحنين كان يسبقوني، ام احبك.

انت التي ربيتيني و تعبتي علي، امي الغالية

Mohamed Assaf (12)

My Poem

My poem
is a plate of hot spicy dahl
a smell that fills my nostrils
and consumes me into its powerful pungent wrath
the hot polluted air of the place I lived in
like a leech sucking the air out of me.
Hmm . . . no matter.

My poem
burns the tip of my tongue
But as I'm told 'patience is a virtue'
and I have little of it.
It's trees that produce sweet dark fluid
It's sap that fabricates
a hard dull block of molasses.

My poem
feels like small rocks being pulled by a wave
ebbing slowly in an ocean tide.
It is the young farmers in a watery land
under the intense heat,
being wrapped in a cloak of frustration and hunger
and so

my poem is my country,
my home country.
And my country is poor.

Tarzina Khatun (16)

To the Taliban

I haven't been to your hell
for terrorising, theft, or treachery,
for stealing young boys and girls.
But I have heard your thundery shootings,
the yells of children,
the cries of hearts.

I haven't touched your grenades or your bullets;
nor worn your chain of bullets around my neck
and claimed jihad;
but I have touched broken lives,
shattered glass,
and walked on an injured land,
where blood oozes and boils
until the steam reaches your nostrils.

I haven't read the Quran you have read
where to kill is fine
where rape is acceptable.
But I have read the Quran of Prophet Mohammad (PBUH)
where killing one person is killing all of humanity.

I haven't felt the texture of your hairy face,
your stained clothes
stained with bloodshed
stained with sins,
heavy with all
that is pulling you down.

I have felt the texture
of the man's white face that you killed.
It was like the touch of a cloud.
My eyes glitter with the shine of the martyrs.

Shukria Rezaei (18)

Black Cheetos

Can I touch your hair? She asks you as she bites her lip, pupils dilating with excitement. Your hands stop others when they ghost over your tight black curls. You don't even make eye contact. You just stop them in their tracks before they do any damage. You apologise for your sudden aggression after seeing her pout. You explain that it's just a thing. When you have hair that is visibly different, like a 'fro or dreads, you say no when asked for permission to touch. You tell her that it's like a silent tradition that has been passed down generations after generations. You smile as she nods, seeming to understand what you have been telling her. But what you really wanted to say was that without realising it, she was dehumanising you. That she was implying that your hair is exotic, not normal. Maybe even a little like black Cheetos. But you give her props for asking you, normally people would just touch it. Petting you like a dog. Their bacteria filled hands all up your scalp.

Han Sun Nkumu (18)

I am from there

(after Mahmoud Darwish)

I am from there, and I have memories.
I had friends and brothers. I had
a tree around the corner from my house.

Now I have a room and I see from my window
green and cold buildings and birds still in colours.
I remember my brothers, how they died.

I want to forget everything; I know I must look
to my future. I remember I walked and crossed
the land and the sea when I came from there.

I learned all the world, yet I only remember
the tears of my brothers as they came down.
When I saw the blood on my brother's body.

I cannot forget this scene.

Einas Hadla (18)

I Come From

I come from a land where the earth's beauty
seems like a myth. The smell of perfume
trying to mask the smell of the overflowing bins,
where I can smell my mother's cooking a mile away.

I come from a place where I can hear myself speak
through the mouths of others. A place where you can feel
the thump of the talking drum, the steady sound of static TV.
Where my aunt quarrels in a language I do not understand.

I come from a family of a thousand relatives, of nurses
and drivers of buses, where you can never count
your cousins and nieces. Where school and education
are tightly grabbed onto, where parents' expectations

are shouted through the roofs; where *we will survive*
is a line to get you up in the morning,
and *hardship makes you a man* is a lullaby.
But I am a boy, who wants to stay a boy.

I come from corruption and poverty
poverty like the smell
of a man's sweet meaninglessness.

I come from love and affection.
A flame that can't be put out.
A warmth that grooms me.

Michael Egbe (17)

My Worst Habit

My worst habit is drinking too much
nostalgia,
until it becomes bittersweet
like the bottom of a tea glass.

My past seems rosy
yet, afraid to go back,
my thoughts lose clarity,
I get tangled, knotted up in wonder.

How to cure nostalgia? Give it
a chance to relieve your pressure.
How to cure a bad habit?
Send it back to yourself.

Don't let nostalgia tighten
your throat. Take sips
of your memories
all day and all night.

Shukria Rezaei (18)

My Dad Cooks the World and his Past
in a Steam Cooker

I eye him in the kitchen,
watch him build a plate of food
before he's even
cut the garlic, line up

the wooden spoons like the doors
of the past. Recipes
from his childhood
haunt him, and the places

he was taught to chop
the tomatoes and the onions,
and scald the pan. Nothing
ever tastes as good

as the first time he made it,
back home. The beans he soaks
in water and the rice
he bathes in a steamy pot.

The garden is his Columbian market
now. The weeds hassle
the green stalks on their way,
and hold hands with the apple tree.

My dad is a resurrector
of beans, a puller-back
of dead skins, a conductor
of vegetable stew.

When he serves it to me
he smiles and I know
that if the food is good
his day was good,

because life is good when the food is.

Aisha Borja (15)

Iman Dari

Iman Dari: I don't have it

When India split
new languages formed
rich languages
Words meaning *truth, trust, tearful*
split.
I swear by God she said
Don't take God's name in vain

Iman Dari – In our family
there are many sides, shades, colours to it.
Iman Dari my brother yells:
I haven't seen it,
I didn't take it.
Iman Dari I saw you take it.
Well, I forgot.

Iman Dari I can smell the *Nihari*
I can hear the *Azaan,* louder
than the street vendors
Iman Dari I can.
I know it's *Namaz* time
though I can't hear the *Moazin*
It's England.
My ears are ringing.
I'm only hearing the *Azaan* in my mind.

Iman Dari I say, in my heart.

Maah-Noor Ali (17)

When I Came from Nepal

As I clutched my suitcase
thick hot sweat built up
in the slits of my palms, which
shook holding its cool
metal brace. We walked
into day-winds, thick
as dried out paint
on unwashed brown canvases.
The sky was painted daffodil yellow.
The floor was a dirty grey.
There was a metal bird:
an array of fearful,
forgotten
paint.

*

I smell the iron rust
of the Municipal Gardens.
The sour tang of home still
sits on the tip of my tongue
like the zest of sweet citrus
fizzing.

*

I did not know
of grey, gravel roads,
or the bright buzzing,
of scarlet cars.
I did not know
of lonely red-bricked houses,
gazing strangers,
standing next to next,
military officers, in endless rows.
I did not know,
of silence in the streets,
or the secret whispers on the buses,
or the sly gestures of restaurants.

In this place,
where I did not know,
the things I did not know
embrace me in ways
I didn't know.

Mukahang Limbu (15)

Korean Festival Mask

I am from Korea.
Don't ask if it's North or South.
I was there before it was separated.

I don't know what my owner was
but from the way his finger traced
each part of my dragon face

delicately, I think: a gentle person.
Each year, he took me out of the darkness
and into the freshness of the new year's spring.

If you were to pick me up, put me on,
let my jaw move, freely
I would tell you that story again.

The story of the snow melting
to welcome spring. And how
Buddha has aged another year.

Han Sun Nkumu (17)

Bridge

Between here and Colombia
is a pontoon
of fishnet tights filled tight
with star fruit and green, salted mango.

From here to Colombia
is a pageant
of carnivals and parties
and 1am celebrations and girls
in homemade wedding dresses
twirling on their great-great-uncle's toes.

Between here and Colombia
is a green wave
of parrots tumbling in cages no bigger
than their beady, red-glass eyes.

From here to Colombia
is a necklace
of gourds frothing
with brown nameless soups and fried
everything and big bottom ants and
sauces from everywhere and roadkill armadillo.

Between here and Colombia
is a zip line
of stretched elastic marriages
to high school boyfriends.

Between here and Colombia
are stepping stones
of thousands of lost relatives weaving
down hot pavements dangerous with carts
ready to pinch your cheeks and say
You are too thin, what have you been doing?

And I will set out to travel
from here to Colombia
I shall step out
onto the stretched-tight washing line
which links our houses
and wobble onto
the telephone wires
which dangle in the mango trees.
I will ignore the calls
from great-aunts and great-grandmas
great-cousins and first cousins,
and hold out the corners of my dancing skirt.
I shall point my jelly sandals
towards the Columbian sun
and dance *cumbia, cumbia* –

until I get there.

Aisha Borja (15)

Parallel

I whisper to myself,

frozen in a faded photograph,
a girl with my features but smaller,
pigtails and a wide, honest smile.
I tell her about it.

From a room of clean-painted walls
she laughs back at me,
and I tell her about the grey roads
and the pale, whitewashed skies.

I tell her she'll get taller
and that her hair will be cut short
like her time spent smiling.
I tell her a tale of giants

wrapped in purple: faces blurred,
careless features. I show her
through my telescope
the patterns of the ghastly wind

whispering lies that will echo
with the thunder of a storm
and strike with the power of its lightning.
I take her to the shore

and we swing back and forth
to the pulse of the waves
licking the dry sand
in a heartbeat.

She takes me back
to a garden full of spring
and picks me forget-me-nots.
She whispers in my ear

The secrets I half-forgot.
I hold a piece of paper
and I watch the tip of my pen
leave a mark.

Now the room smells of tangled parallels
and forget-me-nots.

Vivien Urban (17)

A Girl is Told to Always Keep Writing

Some people burn their poetry into their skin,
Swallow it at meals till their lips are mangled yellow from fire.
I see their blazing eyes and dream ways to begin
Is being a fan an insult? It's them I admire.

They are living on a stage,
While dust and unspoken words fill my lungs.
They burn in the most beautiful way.
I am writing a song I know won't be sung.

I am a girl breathing dirt from the floor,
In a race to be Something or Anything before
I die. Before the pale grey sky can wrap around me
Like a coat and stop me breathing.

I sit twisting my notebook pages
Into spirals. Not minding that the ink fades.

Jasmine Burgess (15)

I Shall Go Back

I shall put the suitcase full of gifts
I have promised, down on the floor.
The gifts they have been waiting for.
I shall see their smiles.

I shall hang the flowers
that my cousins, uncles, and aunties
have put around my neck at the airport,
on the nail.

I shall sit down for dinner,
with family
and breathe the steam of *Quadid*
that nourishes you just by its smell.

I shall sleep outside,
in the hot summer night
and feel the soft winds holding me
and I shall never
wake up with the fear of war.

I shall hear my mum swooshing the carpet-sweeper
early in the morning.
I shall hear her say: *Wake up, guests*
are coming. The house needs to be tidy.

I shall feel at home, once again.

Shukria Rezaei (16)

Home

I miss being in the land
where I was born and grew up.
Our dreams are there
but my destiny is not to be
with Damascus who gave me my soul.
Damascus where the sun rises in my room
and the birds sing at my window.

Damascus, my mother.

Mohamed Assaf (12)

The Path

I know the people on this path:

I know who were vagabond,
but now are returning home; I know
who are losing their home; who
walk in front of me
with only one place to go.

I know who are like me:
I know they want to stay
in between the rain and the sun
on the path that begins
with the moon but ends with the sun.

I know what it's like
to only half-understand
the words people say, to half-
belong in a room. I know
what it is to be in between.

Sophie Dunsby (17)

Of Colour

My
words have to
have
colour

the colour of skies.
of girls in yellow coats –
            of the skins of dumplings peeled by
                                steam kisses
the shades of snot sneezed
into
blue
hankies –

                colour

                    of dead skin scrubbed by
                        hands of dusk –
of unwashed teacups, of unwashed socks.
Shades of
hummingbirds across hijabs,

                        of Christian girls

in

                    silver boots.

The colours
of mothers who kiss hands –
of mothers who God forbade to
read.

Mukahang Limbu (16)

Origins

In my country:
I felt the rough sand
scrub against my feet;
chased salty orange crabs
who pinched my pinkie tight;
so by firelight,
I would crunch into lemon-seeping shells,
feel the faint texture of sand resting on my tongue.

In my other country:
I fell in love with the pitter-patter
of sticks on a drum; the click-clack
of polished shoes on the wooden floor,
the sweaty palms as we danced,
the bagpipes, and the deafening sound from the band.

I grew up here:
with red mud squelching between my toes,
with warm sand colouring my feet white,
and the cool sea washing them clean.

I grew up here:
resting under the palm trees
drinking *Dafu* juice,
snoozing on the *Baraza* beneath the stars.

I grew up here: in the *Gorbals*,
with Kwiksave, the Junkies,
and chucking snowballs;

watching fireworks
on the eighth floor of my council flat,
listening to the bangs and cracks;
watching the orange flames
flower out.

Azfa Awad (18)

My Mother Country

I don't remember her
in the summer,
lagoon water sizzling,
the kingfisher leaping,
or even the sweet honey mangoes,
they tell me I used to love.
I don't remember
her comforting garment,
her saps of date trees,
providing the meagre earnings,
for those farmers
out there
in the gulf
under the calidity of the sun,
or the mosquitoes,
droning in the monsoon,
or the tipa tapa of the rain,
on the tin roofs,
dripping on the window,
I think.

Rukiya Khatun (17)

The Poets

ISMAIL AKTHAR is a quiet, bright, respectful Bangladeshi boy, now sixteen. He is not generally a poet, but this anguished howl, produced one sunny afternoon in Year 7, is certainly a poem.

MAAH-NOOR ALI is a delicate, elegant, thoughtful young person, prone to lengthy bouts of self-doubt. She summoned herself more and more through her school days and is now studying English at Oxford.

MOHAMED ASSAF wrote the poems here when he was just twelve years old: a tiny, strikingly beautiful boy from Syria. In English, and in school, Mohamed is wild and naughty, manners learned perhaps during his long sojourn in Lebanon, but an older Arabic poet lives inside him.

AZFA AWAD was sixteen when I first met her, and feeling lost after dislocating moves first from her own country, then from Glasgow. Her gift for poetry and rhetoric, though, was very pronounced and she was soon writing independently. She won the prestigious Tower Poetry Prize, studied Creative Writing at Warwick, met the Queen, and is now a fully-fledged poet and performer. Her show *Map of Me* toured the UK in 2016, and she may be contacted at azfaawad.com

MIRON BARTOWSKI was a quiet, small Polish boy with an attentive ear for assonance and a thoughtful eye for images who blossomed suddenly into a tall, blond dream-boat. His subsequent swanning round Year 10 was enhanced by his reputation as a soulful poet.

EMEE BEGUM moved from Bangladesh when she was ten, having had no formal education, and her gloriously open, child-like poems speak directly from that dislocation. She went on to university with the intention of teaching.

AISHA BORJA comes from the Columbia of her father's family, and the otherness of profound dyslexia. Her images marinate a long time in her head before she can write them down, and the gifted results have won her the Foyle Competition and First Story National Writer's Award. Everything but poetry at school continues to be very hard for Aisha but she always retains her cheer and humour.

JASMINE BURGESS comes from an Asian/British heritage, and the isolation of early deafness. She is as gifted in maths as she is in writing. She won the Foyle Competition when she was just thirteen, and gained an A* in A Level Creative Writing at fifteen.

ANTON CHRAPOVIKIJ is a computer scientist, really, but liked a bit of creative writing. This poem, like all his best work, gives us a little of his Russian hinterland.

SOPHIE DUNSBY is from a mixed Filipino/British family, and the younger sibling of triplets. Sophie is a prose-writer, really: her delicate, ironical stories, with their wrenchingly lost, gender-fluid protagonists, will surely be published soon. For the present, she is studying at Bath Spa University.

MICHAEL EGBE came from Nigeria when he was twelve. At school, he was a ball of talent and chaos, as likely to write an extraordinary poem as he was to write nothing; to dance the tango as to lose all his art homework. Mr Dixon taught him to play the piano, Ms

Dix found the art coursework, Ms Aspinall put up with all the drama, and we got him into Liverpool Hope to study performing arts, where he flourishes.

EINAS HADLA arrived in Oxford in 2016 at the age of eighteen, traumatized by the destruction of her family in Damascus. She started to write poetry in Arabic, and transitioned in just a few months to the marvellous Arabic-inflected English you see here.

AMINEH ABOU KERECH and FTOUN ABOU KERECH are sisters, a year apart in age, from Damascus. They arrived in Oxford in 2016 after a long exile in Egypt, and, at once supporting and jostling each other, energetically set about learning English and getting to the top of every class. Their poetry is a joint project: they write all the time, in Arabic and in English, always calling up their homeland.

RUKIYA KHATUN is from Bangladesh, a quiet, veiled girl with a quiet, spiritual presence and a gentle manner. She is, however, formidably determined: arriving in this country at the age of six, she made her way through a rocky series of schools all the way to being called to the Bar in 2017. Her exquisite poems, always calling up that early loss of language and country, were an inspiration when she wrote them and remain one of my great delights.

TARZINA KHATUN is Rukiya's beautiful, out-going, though still dutiful, younger sister. The poem here shows her more conflicted, and political, feelings about her home country.

MUKAHANG LIMBU is the most artistic and extraordinary of all our school's population of mannerly, motivated Nepalese students. The child of a very young single mother, he arrived in England when he was six, and made his home in study and in theatre. Mukahang is gifted in music, theatre, and the making of friendships as well as writing.

HALEMA MALAK is the only daughter in a house of brothers. A Pashtu speaker, she came to England from Afghanistan when she was ten. She had no formal education, but has taken to English voraciously, writing novels as well as poems.

HAN SUN NKUMU has a complex identity as a black Korean British person. Artistic as well as poetic, she has returned to Korea to study.

ASIMA QAYYUM came from Pakistan when she was three with her large family. Her remarkable prose memoir, *The Cowley Road*, can be read online in the journal of interrupted studies. It records the personal and intellectual development of a tender, joyous, inquiring mind. Asima longs to go to university, something she cannot do until her visa problems are finally resolved.

RABIA REHMEN is the immensely hard-working and supportive daughter of a disabled Pakistani widow. After a childhood of bereavement and frequent moves, she settled both in Oxford and at school, and is currently studying urban design and planning.

SHUKRIA REZAEI arrived in Oxford at fourteen, a refugee from Taliban persecution of her Hazara people in the Pakistan border regions of Afghanistan. Contained, careful, and ironical, Shukria started writing poems in English almost before she had the words to do so, bringing a gift for image and rhetorical vehemence from her Persian heritage. Over four years, she developed into a truly remarkable poet, and has seen her work published in *Oxford Poetry* among others.

VIVIEN URBAN arrived from Hungary in Year 7, a studious, earnest village girl in plaits. Seven years later, she was Prom Queen and Head Girl, a brilliant student and shining beauty. Her poems reflect her intellect and acute interest in language. She is studying English, Languages, and Creative Writing at St Andrews.

THE EDITOR

KATE CLANCHY was born and grew up in Scotland. She is a writer in several genres, and has won the BBC National Short Story Award for her fiction, a Forward Prize and the Saltire Prize for her poetry, and the Writers' Guild Award for her much acclaimed memoir *Antigona and Me*. She was shortlisted for the Ted Hughes Award for *We Are Writing a Poem About Home*, a radio poem by the students of Oxford Spires Academy where she has been Writer in Residence since 2009.

Supporting poetry through this book

A donation of 50p from the sale of this book will be made to and shared equally between the charities First Story and Forward Arts Foundation, who have backed Kate Clanchy's work in OSA.

First Story first placed her in the school in 2009 and supported her residency there for six years. It continues to place acclaimed writers in secondary schools serving low-income areas across the country: you can read about its work on https://www.firststory.org.uk/

Forward Arts Foundation continues to support Kate and her students with funds, books and advocacy: it promotes poetry excellence through programmes including the Forward Prizes for Poetry and National Poetry Day.

A Note on Translation

Some poems by our Syrian poets, Mohammed Assaf and Amineh Abou Kerech, were originally written in Arabic and translated by distinguished academics Ala Owaineh, Julia Bray, Mohamed-Salah Omri, for which are very grateful.

ACKNOWLEDGEMENTS

Thank you

To some extraordinary teachers: Emma Bate, Helen Woolley, Helen Beech, Christine Atkinson, Linda Woodley, Trish Thornhill, Jackie Watson, and Andrew Archibald, and two fantastic librarians, Katherine Whittington and James Shepherd, for everything they have done in Oxford Spires. This is a team effort and you are the team.

To Iona Fabian, for filming us.

To Sue Croft, Headteacher, for investing in me and believing in me and in the value of the arts in school.

To Alan Buckley, for unfailing collegiate support.

To Stephen Matthews, Niall Munro and Simon Kovesi at Brookes for the Oxford City Poet scheme and everything else they have done for me and my poets over many years.

To Matthew Reynolds, Katrin Khol and the OWRI Team for the new excitement of the home languages poetry initiative.

To Azfa Awad and Shukria Rezaei for the special, extra years.

To Susannah Herbert at the Forward Arts Foundation for her unfailing interest, her investment, her humour and kindness – you saved me.

To Monica Parle, Katie Waldegrave and Will Fiennes at First Story for putting me in school in the first place, royal visits, and all sorts of other support.

To Don Paterson, Paul Baggaley, and all at Picador, and Zoe Waldie at RCW for believing in this book.